JOSHUA MILLS

atmosphere

Creating a Realm
for Miracles & Success!

Atmosphere: Creating a Realm for Miracles & Success

ISBN: 978-0-9830789-4-4

Copyright © 2011 by Joshua Mills

Published by New Wine International, Inc.
www.NewWineInternational.org

Cover design by Ken Vail at www.prevailcreative.com
Internal design by David Sluka and Ronald Olson

Printed in the United States of America

Note: This book is not intended to provide or take the place of medical advice or treatment from your personal physician. You are advised to consult your own doctors or other qualified health professionals regarding the treatment of your medical conditions. Neither the publisher nor the author takes any responsibility for any possible consequences from any treatment, action, or medical application to any person reading or following the information in this book.

Endorsements

✝ *"This is the book you've been waiting for!! Joshua Mills' concise yet practical applications for sustaining God's glory, presence, victory and atmosphere will change your life! This timely, informative book will help you realize your position in Christ and encourage you to examine the way you think about your walk with God. This is your handbook for the good life, the God life!"*

Steve Swanson
Friends Of The Bridegroom Worship Ministries
Casa Grande, Arizona
www.fobworshipmin.org

✝ *"ATMOSPHERE by Joshua Mills is packed with thought-provoking, ministry-impacting revelation. This easy read is a MUST for any Spirit-led worship leader."*

LaRue Howard
Recording Artist/Music Pastor
New Beginnings Church
Orlando, Florida

✝ *"As a worship leader and pastor, I know that creating an atmosphere charged with the Holy Spirit is the foundation to seeing lives and hearts transformed.*

Joshua has taken an experience that many people long for and lays out truth and revelation on how to facilitate and live in an atmosphere of the Glory Realm. If you desire to see God's presence engulf every aspect of your life and ministry, ATMOSPHERE *is your key."*

Kelley Warren Augi
Worship Pastor, Dominion Outreach Centre
Ottawa, Ontario, Canada
www.robertandkelley.com

✝ *"Joshua Mills has put together with profound simplicity, guidelines for creating an environment that will aid any individual in pursuit of their highest potential in God. He takes us from the basics we have forgotten to fresh understanding of how to position ourselves to receive revelation. You will enjoy learning how to create your desired atmosphere in which you can discover untapped creativity as you detangle yourself from the things around you that are drain-*

ing your energy, thoughts, time, and resources. Easy to understand and very accessible!"

JoAnn McFatter
Inside Eternity Ministries
Foley, Alabama
www.joannmcfatter.com

✝ *"It's no accident that wherever Joshua Mills ministers the atmosphere around him begins to change and all kinds of miracles and manifestations take place. In this book, Joshua will equip you with powerful truths for living a sustainable supernatural lifestyle and seeing your environment completely transformed! Read with great expectation and get ready to soar into new dimensions of freedom found in the Glory Realm."*

Bonnie Whaley
Integrity Music Artist and Worship Leader
City Church International,
Hong Kong, Hong Kong
www.bonniewhaley.com

Dedication

These revelations have been stirring inside my spirit for quite a few years, and I have even taught an entire lesson on "Building The Realm." But it wasn't until I was recently teaching *The School Of Miracles* at Victory Christian Center in Houston, Texas, that the students pulled these truths from my spirit, which caused me to sit down and write these things on paper.

I therefore want to dedicate this book to Pastor Tony Krishack and his entire leadership team for their persistence in pursuing the glory of God and creating a realm for miracles and success in their sphere of influence.

Thank You

I want to thank Janet Angela and Lincoln for creating an atmosphere of love in our home where I can be creative, write and revelate in the things of God.

Thank you also to my amazing editor, David Sluka, and his team, and my graphic designer, Ken Vail, for their tremendous work.

Contents

Foreword by Dr. Clarice Fluitt 15

Introduction 17

Chapter 1:
20 Facts About Your Atmosphere 19

Chapter 2:
Body, Soul & Spirit 31

Chapter 3:
Creating a Miracle Climate 39

Chapter 4:
Sound & Light 59

Chapter 5:
Colors 67

Chapter 6:
Organization 75

Chapter 7:
Generosity 83

Chapter 8:
Influencing Your Environment..................95

Foreword by Dr. Clarice Fluitt

We have been taught that the *natural atmosphere* speaks of the prevailing influence or *spirit* surrounding the *air* in any given space. Webster also defines it as a thrilling and often exotic or heady effect that can produce a *mood change* through music, decorations, color, art, etc. But we also know there is the *supernatural presence* of the Glory of God that always creates a disruption in our natural atmosphere and produces an *eternal change in our lives.*

Joshua Mills is an atmosphere changer! He has his *spiritual thermostat* on the *red-hot Glory setting* and he obviously has decided to agree with God to live the life of a worshipping miracle worker.

Joshua is a weapon of righteousness in the hands of a mighty God. As you read this book it will inform and transform your life and *you, too,* can become an atmosphere changer.

Dr. Clarice Fluitt
Founder and Co-Pastor, Eagles Nest Church
World Prayer and Training Center, Monroe, Louisiana

Introduction

As I HAVE TRAVELED AROUND THE WORLD for the past 15 years, I have discovered that atmospheres play a very significant part in understanding how people receive from the presence of God's glory.

I believe that your atmosphere is important to the Lord!

- In the Bible as the angels stirred the waters of Bethesda an atmosphere for healing was released. (See John 5:2-3.)
- An atmosphere for deliverance was created when David the psalmist began to play music upon the harp. (See 1 Samuel 16:23.)
- When the widow gave generously of her last meal, it set into motion an atmosphere for supernatural prosperity that released multiplication into her life. (See 1 Kings 17:7-16.)

God wants to give you an atmosphere for miracles every day of your life!

I believe that I have been given a mandate from the Lord to share these supernatural revelations about creating an atmosphere for miracles so that you will be able to function in your utmost ability and demonstrate the glory realm here on earth.

I know you will be blessed through this book. May the revelatory realms of heaven surround you as you read!

In His Great Love,
Joshua Mills

Chapter 1

20 Facts About Your Atmosphere

"You are the light of the world. A city on a hill cannot be hidden. Neither do people light a lamp and put it under a bowl. Instead they put it on its stand, and it gives light to everyone in the house. In the same way, let your light shine before men, that they may see your good deeds and praise your Father in heaven."

Matthew 5:14-16

Y OUR ATMOSPHERE IS IMPORTANT TO GOD. You were created in an atmosphere of glory and God has always intended for you to live and walk in that dimension of supernatural life. Through the Scriptures we understand that we are "the light of the world." Our atmosphere should reflect this light. And it should cause others around us to praise God and give glory to Him for His everlasting greatness.

In this chapter I want you to see the importance of your atmosphere and how it can either benefit you or hinder you, depending upon the atmosphere you create. You were created for an atmosphere of blessing, life and miracles. You were created for an atmosphere of glory!

1. A Specific Atmosphere Is Necessary For Creativity

Every artist prepares their workspace with proper lighting, music that sets a mood and materials they will use to create, before they begin working on their masterpiece. Oftentimes, these things must be in place in order for the thoughts and ideas from their imagination to appear on the canvas. In the beginning God spoke His "light" into existence before He began working on His magnum opus. In Matthew 21:12, Jesus was bothered by the atmosphere created in the temple because it distracted people from a spiritual focus. The right atmosphere will create the right rewards. *"But when you pray,*

go into your room, close the door and pray to your Father,
who is unseen. Then your Father, who sees what is done in
secret, will reward you" (Matthew 6:6).

2. Your Atmosphere Will Determine Your Fruitfulness

Every harvest is subject to both the seed and the soil. The proper atmosphere will create fertile ground for the seeds you plant. *"Other seed fell among thorns, which grew up and choked the plants, so that they did not bear grain. Still other seed fell on good soil. It came up, grew and produced a crop, multiplying thirty, sixty, or even a hundred times"* (Mark 4:7-8).

3. Atmosphere Will Influence Decisions

Whatever surrounds your life eventually affects your spirit, soul and body. Develop an atmosphere that releases heavenly inspiration and wise counsel. *"Your eye is the lamp of your body. When your eyes are good, your whole body also is full of light. But when they are bad, your body also is full of darkness"* (Luke 11:34).

4. Anointed Music Is Able To Create An Atmosphere Of Serenity, Peace, And Tranquil Rest

The right music may be the key you've been looking for to establish the right atmosphere for success. Many people have told us that our *SpiritSpa* CDs have enabled children to stay focused, helped them become creative, and also brought peace into unsettling situations. People have also used the *SpiritSpa* CD in medical offices, hospitals and clinics in order to promote an atmosphere for healing. It has worked wonders! *"You are my hiding place; you will protect me from trouble and surround me with songs of deliverance"* (Psalm 32:7).

5. Your Atmosphere Is Always Subject To Change

Create an atmosphere of glory and stand on guard, being careful not to allow unwanted parasites from taking over. *"Be sober-minded; be watchful. Your adversary the devil prowls around like a roaring lion, seeking someone to devour"* (1 Peter 5:8).

6. An Outward Atmosphere Will Influence An Inward Atmosphere.

Colors affect your emotional attitude. Spiritual atmosphere will affect your spiritual alertness. Your friends will determine your mindsets, your actions and oftentimes your successes. It is a popular saying that "you become who you hang out with" because it is natural for every human being to be influenced by their environment. Teenagers who become close friends with drug addicts often become druggies themselves. Young people who find a mentor in an accomplished business

It is natural for every human being to be influenced by their environment.

person, often become wealthy business owners, as well. Ministers who hang around with other anointed ministers will discover a greater glory increasing in their own life. One key for creating a dynamic atmosphere for success is to learn how to "hang out with people that are better than you." *"After the Feast was over, while his parents were returning home, the boy Jesus stayed behind in Jerusalem, but they were unaware of it... After three days they found him in the temple courts, sitting among the teachers, listening to them and asking them questions"* (Luke 2:43, 46).

7. An Inward Atmosphere Will Influence An Outward Atmosphere.

There's an old saying, "Whatever goes in must come out." It's very important to cultivate your spiritual walk with the Lord because your outward atmosphere will be affected by your inner peace, inner attitude and your intimate relationship with Jesus Christ. *"You brood of vipers, how can you who are evil say anything good? For out of the overflow of the heart the mouth speaks"* (Matthew 12:34).

8. Your Atmosphere Will Determine Your Growth

Faith comes by hearing the Word, anointing comes through impartation of the Word, and spiritual growth comes by spending time in God's presence. Just as a greenhouse creates a climate for the perfect growth of vegetables, fruits and other plants, the atmosphere of

The atmosphere of God's glory creates the ideal environment for you to flourish.

God's glory creates the ideal environment for you to flourish. Every seed needs to be watered by the refreshing river of God's Spirit and bathed by the light of His glory. *"Planted in the house of the Lord, they will flourish in the courts of our God"* (Psalm 92:13).

9. The Colors In Your Atmosphere Will Magnify Your Emotional Strengths Or Weaknesses

Create an atmosphere that is suitable for you and will allow you to become everything you are intended to be. Colors have the ability to attract or distract your attention. *"Look not thou upon the wine when it is red, when it giveth his colour in the cup, when it moveth itself aright"* (Proverbs 23:31 KJV).

10. Only You Can Determine What Atmosphere You Need

Discern, create, and pursue the things you need in order to create an atmosphere suitable for you. *"And God is able to make all grace abound to you, so that in all things at all times, having all that you need, you will abound in every good work"* (2 Corinthians 9:8).

11. Your Atmosphere Will Determine Your Productivity

Sound, color, light and relationships will increase or decrease your ability to achieve your goals. Learn how to create an atmosphere that will increase your ability to work efficiently and become successful. *"Whatever you do, work at it with all your heart, as working for the Lord, not for men"* (Colossians 3:23).

12. Praise Changes The Atmosphere

Thankfulness will create a realm of appreciation and gratitude. The psalmist David understood the miracle of praise and said that it would continually be upon his lips. God's servant Joshua understood a dimension of praise that held the potential to break down walls and establish the victory of God. People blossom and situations become hopeful when praise enters into the picture. *"Enter his gates with thanksgiving and his courts with praise; give thanks to him and praise his name"* (Psalm 100:4).

13. The Right Atmosphere Is Priceless

A financial sacrifice for the right atmosphere will become the greatest investment you have ever made. Successful people know that without

Successful people know that without a great atmosphere, they are unable to produce great results.

a great atmosphere they are unable to produce great results. The benefits of motivation, productivity and creative thinking are invaluable blessings that deserve to be cultivated in your life at any cost. *"A gift opens the way for the giver and ushers him into the presence of the great"* (Proverbs 18:16).

14. Your Atmosphere Will Determine Your Prosperity

What kind of atmosphere have you been creating with your finances? A withholding attitude invites a poverty atmosphere to surround your financial matters, but a spirit of generosity creates an atmosphere for blessings and overflowing prosperity. *"A generous man will prosper; he who refreshes others will himself be refreshed"* (Proverbs 11:25).

15. Great Relationships Will Produce Great Atmospheres

Surrounding yourself with Bible-believing, faith-filled, miracle-anticipating people will create an atmosphere for God's glory to abound in your life. This is why the Scriptures encourage us to *"Let us not give up meeting together, as some are in the habit of doing, but let us encourage one another"* (Hebrews 10:25).

Many well-meaning Christians have stopped going to church because they haven't realized the importance of great relationships. There are no perfect churches, because there are no perfect people! But it is important to get plugged into a local fellowship and join together frequently with others that are like-minded and like-spirited, because a miracle connection will produce a miracle atmosphere! (See 1 Corinthians 15:33 and 1 Thessalonians 5:12.) *"Blessed is the man who does not walk in the counsel of the wicked or stand in the way of sinners or sit in the seat of mockers"* (Psalm 1:1).

16. Atmospheres Can Be Conditioned For The Miraculous

Praise conditions an atmosphere with victory. Prayer conditions an atmosphere with change. Prophecy conditions an atmosphere with potential. Participation conditions an atmosphere with manifestation. When the early believers gathered together in the Upper Room, they conditioned the atmosphere for the miraculous outpouring of the Holy Spirit. *"When the day of Pentecost came, they were all together in one place. Suddenly a sound like the blowing of a violent wind came from heaven and filled the whole house where they were sitting"* (Acts 2:1-2).

17. Your Attitude Will Affect Your Atmosphere

Negative attitudes will create an atmosphere of strife, struggle and loss. The atmosphere that negativity produces will stifle your success. Positive attitudes will create an atmosphere for productivity, motivation and miracles. Be careful to watch the attitude of your heart. Allow God's Word and Spirit to bring hope and healing to your life issues and it will change your attitude. *"You were taught, with regard to your former way of life, to put off your old self, which is being corrupted by its deceitful desires; to be made new in the attitude of your minds"* (Ephesians 4:22-23).

18. Religion Will Bring Destruction To Your Atmosphere

Religious rules and regulations will prevent your atmosphere from flourishing with God's creative potential. Dead religion disregards the grace of God. Jesus Christ wants to have a relationship with you, not a religious ritual (see more on page 49). *"...have you not read what God said to you, 'I am the God of Abraham, the God of Isaac, and the God of Jacob'? He is not the God of the dead but of the living"* (Matthew 22:31-32).

19. God Created You For A Specific Atmosphere

You were born for it, long for it and desire to reach out to attain it. The atmosphere of glory is your home. Pursue it and allow it to touch every area of your life. *"He has made everything beautiful in its time. He has also set eternity in the hearts of men; yet they cannot fathom what God has done from beginning to end"* (Ecclesiastes 3:11).

20. The Atmosphere Of God's Glory Contains An Impartation That Will Revolutionize Your Life

Whatever the glory touches begins to change. When the widow woman in Zarephath gave God's prophet Elijah the last of her flour and oil, the glory touched it and it began to multiply with overflowing abundance. (See 1 Kings 17:7-16.) When the servants at the wedding followed the instructions of Jesus and filled the six empty water pots, the glory touched the water and it changed into supernatural wine. When you yield to the move of the Spirit, God's glory contains an impartation that will revolutionize every area of your life – spirit, soul and body. *"And wherever he went – into villages, towns or countryside – they placed the sick in the marketplaces. They begged him to let them touch even the edge of his cloak, and all who touched him were healed"* (Mark 6:56).

Recommended Resources:

- *The Power Of Your Testimony,* Teaching CD (Item #CD-20)
- *The Power Of The Glory Cloud,* Teaching CD (Item #CD-18)
- *Third Day Prayers* Book (Item #BK-13)

Chapter 2

Body, Soul & Spirit

"May God himself, the God of peace, sanctify you through and through. May your whole spirit, soul and body be kept blameless at the coming of our Lord Jesus Christ."

1 Thessalonians 5:23

G OD HAS CREATED YOU AS A THREE-PART BEING. The Bible makes it clear that first and foremost you are a spirit-being and you have a soul. These two invisible parts are housed within your physical body. I want to explain all three of these aspects of your being a little bit further and show you how they relate to the atmosphere that surrounds your life on a daily basis.

"May God himself, the God of peace, sanctify you through and through.
May your whole spirit, soul and body be kept blameless
at the coming of our Lord Jesus Christ."
1 Thessalonians 5:23

Body

This is the "earth suit" that you wear, which contains your soul and spirit. Within Scripture your body is regarded as the "temple of the Lord" and needs to be cared for in order for you to properly minister and do God's work on the earth. *"...offer your bodies as living sacrifices, holy and pleasing to God--this is your spiritual act of worship"* (Romans 12:1).

Our physical bodies contain the natural senses of sight, smell, touch, taste, hearing and equilibrium. These senses often trigger the soul or can be triggered by emotional reactions from our soulish realm. When considering creating an atmosphere, we must realize that our physical senses will react to a physical atmosphere. It is my firm belief that if we can learn how to calm our physical bodies by creating an atmosphere of comfort, it will be easier for our spirit and soul to receive a touch from the Lord because our body isn't being physically distracted.

I believe that people were created for revival, but they weren't necessarily created for weeks of extended revival meetings. What I mean is that God wants to touch people with the manifestation of His glory, but sometimes our physical restraints can put a damper on the move of God's Spirit. Sitting in old wooden chairs in a hot and humid outdoor tent meeting can sometimes be the most uncomfortable situation, especially after several hours of praise, worship, preaching and ministry.

Now, I'm not saying that God can't move in a place like that – I know He can! I've been in some wonderful outdoor tent meetings that have been absolutely glorious and many people have received an eternal touch from Heaven. There have been times we have seen dramatic signs and wonders and creative miracles in those outdoor meetings.

But, the point that I'm trying to stress here is that if we can learn how to build an atmosphere where physical comfort is achieved, it will help us in the ultimate goal of easing the body and soul, so that the spirit of a person can receive a fresh touch from the Spirit of Glory.

Another example of this is in the home. Many people would like to spend some quiet time with the Lord, reading their Bible and interceding in prayer. But sometimes their homes are so disorganized that they can't even begin to find a place to sit down, let alone find some peace and solitude.

Do you find your life cluttered or uncomfortable? Beginning to look after these small natural details of organization can achieve some great results in the spiritual realm. (I've included more information about this in Chapter 6.)

Soul

This is the place where our mind, will and emotions are located. It is the principality of life, feeling, thought and action. The soul is a distinct entity separate from the physical body and the inner spirit. As seen according to this Scripture in Hebrews, there is a distinct difference between the spirit and the soul of a person. Oftentimes these two are confused. The soul is responsible for the emotional and feeling aspects of a person, while the spirit of a person is the true identity which connects to the Spirit of God. *"For the word of God is living and active. Sharper than any double-edged sword, it penetrates even to dividing soul and spirit, joints and marrow; it judges the thoughts and attitudes of the heart"* (Hebrews 4:12).

Just as I have mentioned earlier in regards to the connection between physical comfort and allowing the body to receive from the Lord, there is also a connection between the soul realm and the emotional reaction to the Spirit of God. If you can learn how to create an atmosphere suitable to calming the soul in order for the voice of God to be heard, it will benefit you greatly.

Here is a list of things that can create a positive or negative emotional reaction:

- Sound and music
- Colors

- Light
- Smell and fragrance

Spirit

This is the core being of who you are. It is the spiritual part of you that will survive beyond death. Your spirit contains a spiritual conscience that is able to discern right from wrong. It is the spirit of man that is illuminated by the Seven Spirits of God as described in Isaiah 11:2: The Spirit of the Lord, The Spirit of Wisdom, The Spirit of Understanding, The Spirit of Counsel, The Spirit of Power, The Spirit of Knowledge, The Spirit of the Fear Of The Lord. *"The lamp of the Lord searches the spirit of a man; it searches out his inmost being"* (Proverbs 20:27).

Your spirit is the part of you that is created to receive an impartation from the Lord. It yearns to be closer to God. It's your spirit that has set you on this journey because it is reaching to receive from the eternal dimension of heaven. You were born from the glory, for the glory, and you long to return to that place of complete unity with God.

Your spirit is the part of you that is created to receive an impartation from the Lord.

Everything that is received by your spirit becomes eternal, because your spirit never dies. The most important atmosphere you can create in your life is a spiritual atmosphere that will release the utmost blessing from the divine supernatural realm.

Here are some important things that will create a wonderful atmosphere of glory in your life:

- A Personal relationship with Jesus Christ (John 3:16)
- The Word of God (Luke 4:4)
- Quiet time for prayer and praise (Matthew 6:6)
- Corporate fellowship with other believers (Hebrews 10:25)

Recommended Resources:

- *Healing For Your Body*, Ministry Card (Item #MC-05)
- *Spirit, Soul & Body*, Ministry Card (Item #MC-24)

Chapter 3

atmosphere

Creating a
Miracle Climate

*"To the angel of the church in Laodicea write:
These are the words of the Amen, the faithful
and true witness, the ruler of God's creation. I
know your deeds, that you are neither cold nor
hot. I wish you were either one or the other! So,
because you are lukewarm – neither hot nor cold
– I am about to spit you out of my mouth."*

Revelation 3:14-16

WHAT IS YOUR SPIRITUAL TEMPERA-
TURE? Are you hot or are you cold?
The opening Scripture passage from
the Book of Revelation gives us an understanding that
God is not impressed by spiritual passivity. God is not
impressed by people who are lukewarm in the spirit, but
God is looking for some "red hot" Christians that know
how to live in a climate of glory.

In my travels I've met some very well-meaning
Christian people who go from church to church with
their spiritual finger in the air "detecting" the spiritual
temperature. I've heard some people say things like "Oh,
that church over there is very hot spiritually," or things
like "Oh, no, you would never want to go minister in
that town; it is so spiritually cold." But, I want to tell
you that God has not called you to be a thermometer
in the Spirit. Within the Bible we do not find the Lord
ever asking us to make our pious comments or judg-
mental remarks about other churches, fellowships, de-
nominations or geographical regions. You're not called
to be a thermometer, but you have been called to be a
thermostat.

According to the dictionary definition, a thermostat is a device that maintains a system at a constant
temperature. The thermostat is very aware of the outward temperature, but you see, that is not the focus. The

thermostat is concentrated on changing the atmosphere and it decides where the temperature is going to end up. If the temperature is cold outside, the thermostat is responsible for increasing the heat inside and dictating the way it is going to feel.

Many times we've piously made comments about the coldness of other people's hearts, not realizing that God has given us the responsibility to set the temperature for on-fire revival. If nobody else wants revival, YOU can become the revival! If nobody else wants a move of God, YOU can begin moving with God! If nobody else wants to discover new realms

> *God has given us the responsibility to set the temperature for on-fire revival.*

of Glory, YOU can become the manifestation of God's goodness here on the earth and walk in that glory every single day of your life!

Don't complain any longer about the circumstances that other people have determined for you. Determine, instead, to change the atmosphere and create a climate for miracles because you are a spiritual thermostat.

God has put it on my heart to share these revelations about how you can maintain and stay in the glory realm. What God is doing in this day is all about a lifestyle – it's something that you can live in. You don't just have to visit once in a while. The days of mere visitation are soon coming to an end because it's going to become heavenly habitation!

You have been called by God to set the spiritual atmosphere. You have been called by God to set the spiritual climate in your community, in your city, in your geographical region and in your nation. God has given you the ability to liter-

You have been called by God to set the spiritual atmosphere. ally change the climate. The Lord always wants to lift us into experiencing the realms of heaven. He always wants to take us to another place in the glory – a place we have never known in the natural.

> *"However, as it is written: No eye has seen, no ear has heard, no mind has conceived what God has prepared for those who love him. But God has revealed it to us by his Spirit"* (1 Corinthians 2:9-10).

God wants to take you from glory to glory. He takes you from strength to strength. He moves you from one revelation to the next. The Lord wants to lift you up to another dimension, to the next level. But in order to get to that next level, you are going to have to move. Some people get scared of moving because they are scared of the unknown. But you don't have to be afraid when He is the one leading you and moving you.

"The New" is a continual process, just as His mercies are new every morning. Does this contradict the statement that God never changes? No. It just means He is becoming new unto us, and we are discovering new facets of His mercy and grace. We are the ones seeing Him in a new dimension. We're the ones getting a revelation of who He is.

God never changes, but we do. We are the ones being thrust into "The New," being moved into "the New." "The New" is us continually moving, walking, and saying "Open my eyes, Lord, to who you really are." The church has known Him as Savior, Baptizer, Healer and Provider, but it is time for us to know Him as the King of Glory. In other words, everything that He is – the time has come for us to know it!

> *"For in him we live and move and have our being"* (Acts 17:28).

God is calling you to move. Your praise moves you. You cannot praise without being moved. When you truly open up and begin to praise Him, something happens. You are taken from your circumstance, situation, trial and tribulation into the fullness of His presence, into the realm of victory. Your praise is the voice of victory. Your praise is the voice of faith which releases the victory. You cannot praise very long without coming into the fullness of it.

When all of hell is breaking loose, you just stand in the middle of it and lift up a little praise like Paul and Silas (Acts 16). If that doesn't work, then just praise a little longer. Just continue to praise. Continue to press into the manifestation of God's presence with your praise. Don't stop until you begin seeing a change in the atmosphere.

We don't praise Him because of what we're going through, but we praise Him because of where we're going to! When you get a revelation of the price that was paid at Calvary and the victory that was already achieved through the shed blood of Jesus Christ at the cross, you begin to understand that your praise connects you with those blessings. It's your faith lining up to the reality of salvation. Suddenly, your declaration becomes a motivation for the manifestation to become your impartation! Your praise will move you into position and align you with heaven's blessings.

We don't praise Him because of what we're going through, but we praise Him because of where we're going to!

The Lord told me that our praise changes the atmosphere but it's our worship that sustains the realm. In order to move into that new place, we need to begin to praise. Praise needs to become your lifestyle. You need to tell yourself, "Praise is what I do because it's who I am," and "I am a Praise." Just begin to declare it.

You can't talk about praise and be quiet. Your praise will move you into a higher dimension.

> *"Shout for joy to the Lord, all the earth. Worship the Lord with gladness; come before him with joyful songs... Enter his gates with thanksgiving and his courts with praise; give thanks to him and praise his name"* (Psalm 100:1, 2, 4).

Let your praise stir you up and move you and begin to change the atmosphere all around you. Come on – right now – as you're reading this book, just begin to praise the Lord for His greatness and begin to witness your atmosphere changing right now!

Your praise changes your atmosphere, but your worship will sustain the realm.

This is an important revelation to grasp onto because the church, in general, is so used to spiritual warfare and fighting and struggling and striving that we're good at changing the atmosphere, but once it's changed, we walk away and think the job is all done. When we turn around the next day, suddenly we realize that it has all gone back down again. So, we do it all over again. We war and walk away, war and walk away, and it seems to be a never ending struggle.

Get this key right here: the battle is not yours; it belongs to the Lord. In the realm of glory we move from warfare to worship. Our praise changes the atmosphere and then we move into worship where we can sustain the realm, and when it is sustained, it literally creates a climate or a new temperature.

A sustained climate creates a culture and people begin to respond to that culture.

For quite a few years, Janet Angela and I have maintained ministry offices in both Southern California and in Canada. Our ministry offices and home in Southern California are located in the beautiful vacation oasis of Palm Springs. The climate there is sunny, dry and arid, as it is situated within the Coachella Valley, just east of Los Angeles. In Palm Springs we enjoy approximately 354 days of sunshine! Rain is a very unusual and odd rarity, so when it happens, everything closes up and people stay off of the roads. Because of the beautiful sunny climate we have approximately 125 golf courses in the area and quite a few gorgeous resort hotels with large swimming pools. Most of the shopping and leisure activities are located outside because the climate has created an outdoor culture.

A sustained climate creates a culture and people begin to respond to that culture.

Janet Angela and I really enjoy the superb weather and moderate temperatures in the wintertime. It is such an ideal place to live, work and relax. We eat outdoors, we play outdoors, and many times we even work outdoors! Even as I've been writing this book, I've been sitting out on my patio in the sunshine, with a stunning vista of the San Jacinto mountains and surrounded by beautiful palm trees and the smell of fresh citrus fruit growing on my orange trees.

Many other places in Southern California have been blessed by this moderate weather as well, and it has created many cultures. Within this area there is a beach and surfing culture, a culture of health and wholeness with many walking trails, leisure sport activities, and fresh fruits and vegetables available in abundance. You see, the climate creates a culture.

In Canada the temperatures are a bit colder, and this has created a winter culture. This country has been made famous for our hockey, ice skating, skiing, snow-shoeing and other wintertime activities. Where we maintain our full-time residence in Langley, British Columbia, the weather is more moderate than in most other places in Canada.

We are so blessed that our winters are mild with only a rare snowfall and temperatures rarely dipping below 40 degrees Fahrenheit. But as we look out from our home, we are surrounded by massive mountains covered in snow. The world-famous resort town of Whistler is only a short drive up into the mountains, and people from all over the world come here to ski and play in the snow. This climate has also created an entirely different culture of its own.

Our family has been very blessed to travel all over the world, and we have been privileged to meet some of the most amazing people and experience some very diverse and interesting cultures. We have spent a very cold night in minus 65-degree weather in an icy igloo up on the top of the earth in the Canadian Arctic, and we have witnessed the sparkling wonder of dazzling glow worms in the Waitomo Caves of New Zealand on the bottom of the globe.

I have taken a ride on the back of an elephant through the jungles of Sri Lanka and have been blessed to share fresh coffee with the natives in the rainforests of Brazil. And in all of these places you will find one thing in common – all of these people have developed their own unique culture.

In the natural realm, the climate affects the way that people live, eat and celebrate. Their climate is responsible for creating their culture.

In the supernatural realm, God wants us to change the atmosphere with our praise and then sustain that realm with our worship because when the realm is sustained, it creates a temperature and that temperature will ultimately result in a different kind of culture.

There has been a culture of religion in the church and it does nothing but bring confusion and disruption to the move of the Spirit. It causes heartache, pain and division between brother and sister and even division in churches and communities, which ultimately results in a culture of confusion.

> *A culture of religion in the church does nothing but bring confusion and disruption to the move of the Spirit.*

Confusion comes from the enemy, as we see in 1 Corinthians 14:33. The reason religion has not worked is because God has never been a part of it.

7 Facts About The Religious Spirit

1. A Religious Spirit Will Never Allow You To Be Good Enough

It doesn't matter how hard you work, or how much you perform, a religious spirit will never allow you to be "good enough." The enemy will always attempt to rob you of your confidence in Christ. *"Some people are like seed along the path, where the word is sown. As soon as they hear it, Satan comes and takes away the word that was sown in them"* (Mark 4:15).

2. A Religious Spirit Will Make You Work To Death

A religious spirit will tell you that you haven't achieved a closer relationship with the Lord because you haven't worked hard enough for it. In truth, the only way you will be able to have an intimate relationship with the Lord is if you begin to understand the overwhelming miracle of His grace.

God loves you and there is nothing on earth that can change that fact. You can't work for it or earn it. His love is a gift that was completely provided for when Jesus Christ shed His blood on the cross of Calvary. *"Knowing that a man is not justified by the works of the law, but by the faith of Jesus Christ, even we have believed in Jesus Christ, that we might be justified by the faith of Christ, and not by the works of the law: for by the works of the law shall no flesh be justified"* (Galatians 2:16 KJV).

3. A Religious Spirit Will Make False Accusations Against You

You will feel defiled, dirty, ashamed and guilty when a religious spirit tries to attach itself to you. A religious spirit will never allow you to experience the true freedom that comes from the Spirit of God. *"Then I heard a loud voice in heaven say: 'Now have come the salvation and the power and the kingdom of our God, and the authority of his Christ. For the accuser of our brothers, who accuses them before our God day and night, has been hurled down"* (Revelation 12:10).

4. A Religious Spirit Will Stifle Your Creative Ability

All throughout history we can find that whenever a religious spirit was brought into the church, creativity and artistic growth was abolished and dreams were destroyed. God's Spirit is creative in nature and we were formed in His image (Genesis 1:27). In the first chapter of Genesis we read about God creating

> God is still creating things today and He chooses to do it through His people.

the heavens and the earth and He didn't stop there. He is still creating things today and He chooses to do it through His people (Ephesians 2:10).

The Spirit of Glory gives dreams, visions, witty inventions, solutions to problems and the ability to achieve new goals. Jesus is the answer! *"He has filled him with the Spirit of God, with skill, ability and knowledge in all kinds of crafts—to make artistic designs for work in gold, silver and bronze, to cut and set stones, to work in wood and to engage in all kinds of artistic craftsmanship"* (Exodus 35:31-33).

5.   A Religious Spirit Will Stunt Your Growth

Whenever you stop growing, you start dying. This is the calamitous reality of too many Christians that have been caught up with a spirit of religion (see Matthew 23:12). A religious spirit masquerades itself as knowing it all, having it all, and achieving it all, while a true, humble spirit will seek to reach out towards the Spirit of Glory that knows-all, holds-all and understands-all. *"A man's pride brings him low, but a man of lowly spirit gains honor"* (Proverbs 29:23).

6.   A Religious Spirit Will Limit Your Productivity, Your Influence and Your Ability

I have found that a religious spirit will always attempt to waste your time with fruitless deeds and unproductive activities. We find this happening many times within the church, where precious saints become preoccupied with religious nonsense that distracts them from the ultimate commission of Jesus Christ, which is to win souls, heal the sick and set the captives free. We must set our priorities and keep first things first! *"Have nothing to do with the fruitless deeds of darkness, but rather expose them"* (Ephesians 5:11).

7.   A Religious Spirit Is A Rebellious Spirit

A religious spirit always rebels against the finished work of grace. It rebels against the move of the Spirit of Glory. It has always rebelled against Jesus Christ and His teachings and it still continues to do the same today. *"For rebellion is like the sin of divination, and arrogance like the evil of idolatry"* (1 Samuel 15:23).

Creating A Glory Culture

Today, God is calling you to change the atmosphere with your praise and sustain that praise with the atmosphere of worship and create a climate through your worship that will create a temperature and ultimately, result in a culture – not a culture of religion – but a glory culture. A culture of glory creates a climate of miracles. Remember these three keys:

1. Creating A Miracle Atmosphere Must Be A Choice

When you choose life, you choose to walk in the blessings of God's miraculous atmosphere. If you choose to walk in sin, there is a correlation to walking in the deception of the curse. God wants all of His children discovering the power of life and blessing that can only be attained through pursuing the grace of God by faith. *"This day I call heaven and earth as witnesses against you that I have set before you life and death, blessings and curses. Now choose life, so that you and your children may live"* (Deuteronomy 30:19).

2. You Will Receive Whatever Atmosphere You Pursue

As you focus on the things of heaven, the things of heaven will begin to focus on you. As you begin to pursue the God of miracles, you will see Him performing them in your life. *"Come close to God, and God will come close to you. Wash your hands, you sinners; purify your hearts, for your loyalty is divided between God and the world"* (James 4:8, NLT).

3. A Miracle Atmosphere Will Benefit Your Life With Immeasurable Blessings

There are no limitations in the Spirit of God. There is no limit to what you will see or what you can achieve when you walk in the Spirit of Glory and allow the miracle realm to fill every area of your life. *"Now there is at Jerusalem by the sheep market a pool, which is called in the Hebrew tongue Bethesda, having five porches. In these lay a great multitude of impotent folk, of blind, halt, withered, waiting for the moving of the water. For an angel went down at a certain season into the pool, and troubled the water: whosoever then first after the troubling of the water stepped in was made whole of whatsoever disease he had"* (John 5:2-4).

How To Cultivate Your Spiritual Climate

There are five things that will affect your physical and emotional atmosphere in a powerful way. I am going to address each one of these things in the following chapters (sound and light, colors, organization, and generosity). But first I want to share with you some very important keys for cultivating a spiritual climate in order to charge your atmosphere with a miracle realm that will continually surround your life.

1.   Make Room For God Daily

God's greatest desire is to fellowship with you on a daily basis. One word from God is more life changing than a lifetime of man's wisdom. One touch from God has the ability to revolutionize every area of your life. One glimpse of God's glory will change your vision and cause you to see things you have never dreamed possible! Make room for God in your life every day by spending time in prayer, praise or reading His Word. *"Better is one day in your courts than a thousand elsewhere; I would rather be a doorkeeper in the house of my God than dwell in the tents of the wicked"* (Psalm 84:10).

2.   Resist The Enemy

The Scriptures tell us that if we resist the enemy of our soul, he has no choice but to flee. Freedom is a choice! If you want to see the glory of God increase in your life, begin focusing on the good things of God and resist the temptations of the enemy. *"Resist him, standing firm in the faith, because you know that your brothers throughout the world are undergoing the same kind of sufferings"* (1 Peter 5:9).

3. Determine To Access The Miracle Realm By Faith

Faith moves mountains and removes obstacles. It shifts the supernatural into the natural realm. Sing your praises with faith. Read your Bible in faith. Give your financial offerings in faith. Without faith it's impossible to please God, but with faith you become a receiver of heaven's rewards! *"…we have gained access by faith into this grace in which we now stand. And we rejoice in the hope of the glory of God"* (Romans 5:2).

4. Expect The Word Of God To Come Alive In Your Life

Know the Word of God, believe the Word of God, and expect the Word of God to become revealed through your life. Expect the same miracles of the Bible to take place in your life. Jesus Christ is the same yesterday, today and forever! *"For the word of God is living and active. Sharper than any double-edged sword, it penetrates even to dividing soul and spirit, joints and marrow; it judges the thoughts and attitudes of the heart"* (Hebrews 4:12).

5. Allow God To Make Any Necessary Changes In Your Life

Do not resist the changes, but allow God to create new habits, routines, assignments, and thought patterns. God wants you to live in the glory realm and in victory! *"Repent, then, and turn to God, so that your sins may be wiped out, that times of refreshing may come from the Lord"* (Acts 3:19).

6. Celebrate Your Victories And Focus On Your Triumphs

Rejoice and give God praise for the breakthroughs you are experiencing in your life today. They may seem small right now, but as you focus on them they will grow and increase. Do not "pray your problems" but praise God for your victories and you will see them overtake every area of your life. *"But thanks be to God! He gives us the victory through our Lord Jesus Christ"* (1 Corinthians 15:57).

7. Never Make Any Important Decisions Until You Have Encountered God's Glory

Within God's glory is the realm of direction, success and overflowing blessing. Bring all of your important decisions to God and allow Him to give you His perfect peace with an answer. The difference between a "good idea" or a "God idea" could mean success or failure. "God ideas" always succeed! *"He will call upon me, and I will answer him; I will be with him in trouble, I will deliver him and honor him. With long life will I satisfy him and show him my salvation"* (Psalm 91:15-16).

Can you feel something stirring inside of you as you read this book? Can you feel the atmosphere shifting as this revelation is unfolding? I know by the Spirit that God wants to release a revelation of His glory into your heart like never before.

YOU can be the one who will manifest the Glory. YOU can be the one who will become an open portal of glory in the earth. YOU can be the one to carry the move of God throughout your spheres of influence. YOU can be the one to manifest the miracles, signs, and wonders. YOU can develop an atmosphere of glory and create a climate for miracles!

Recommended Resources:

- *Carry Your Climate*, Teaching CD (Item #CD-05)
- *7 Secrets For Abiding In The Glory Cloud*, Ministry Card (Item #MC-23)
- *10 Benefits Of Abiding In The Glory Cloud*, Ministry Card (Item #MC-22)

Chapter 4

Sound & Light

"Suddenly a sound like the blowing of a violent wind came from heaven and filled the whole house where they were sitting. They saw what seemed to be tongues of fire that separated and came to rest on each of them."

Acts 2:2-3

I N THE NEW TESTAMENT ACCOUNT from the Upper Room, we discover that the sound and light of God's presence were involved in releasing great power into the atmosphere. The sound of God's mighty rushing wind, and the visible light of His fire released an impartation into the atmosphere for everybody present to receive the infilling of the Holy Spirit.

There is a connection between sound and light. Throughout the Scriptures we can see a spiritual connection, even from the very beginning as God spoke and created instant light (Genesis 1:3). Sound and light will influence your spirit in a powerful manner. Consider these Scripture verses:

> *"The tongue has the power of life and death, and those who love it will eat its fruit"* (Proverbs 18:21).

> *"But if we walk in the light, as he is in the light, we have fellowship with one another, and the blood of Jesus, his Son, purifies us from all sin"* (1 John 1:7).

> *"An evil man is trapped by his sinful talk, but a righteous man escapes trouble"* (Proverbs 12:13).

"...let your light shine before men, that they may see your good deeds and praise your Father in heaven" (Matthew 5:16).

"From the fruit of his lips a man enjoys good things..." (Proverbs 13:2).

"He who guards his mouth and his tongue keeps himself from calamity" (Proverbs 21:23).

In the natural, sound and light are also creative forces that affect your body and mind in a very real way.

1. Sound Has The Ability To Create Healing Within Your Body

High notes correlate with the central nervous system, while notes on the low end of the musical scale deal with the circulatory and blood systems. It's a medical fact that peaceful music assists in reducing stress, and it can help people control the symptoms of illness and disease, even sometimes leading to entirely removing pain from the body. Studies have shown that music therapy can be four to eight times more effective than tranquilizers in reducing the effects of stress, and that it can also lower blood pressure, improve sleep and reduce anxiety.

The ancients believed that music had the power to cure mental disorders and severe depression. According to Scripture, an evil spirit came to King Saul with a physical pain, an emotional torment, and as a spiritual attack that affected his body, mind and spirit. The sound of David's harp caused the evil spirit to depart. *"And whenever the tormenting spirit troubled Saul, David would play the harp. Then Saul would feel better, and the tormenting spirit would go away"* (1 Samuel 16:23).

2. The Correct Use Of Light Creates Specific Moods

Within the context of interior design, light is an element which should not only be used for visual comfort, but also to achieve deliberate emotional responses from as a result of the lighted environment. Light has the ability to create an atmosphere that sparks the soul. Bright levels of lighting produce cheerful effects and encourage people to alertness and activity. On the other hand, low lighting levels tend to create an atmosphere of peace, serenity, relaxation and intimacy. *"The Lord is my light and my salvation – whom shall I fear? The Lord is the stronghold of my life – of whom shall I be afraid?"* (Psalm 27:1).

3. Your Emotions Are Affected By The Sounds You Hear

The part of your brain involved in musical awareness is closely linked to the part that controls your emotions. Slower musical beats can slow your brain waves down and induce relaxation, while faster beats can stimulate the brain. Studies have found that termites will eat wood two times faster when listening to heavy metal music because they become agitated by the sound. *"The Lord is my shepherd, I shall not be in want. He makes me lie down in green pastures, he leads me beside quiet waters, he restores my soul..."* (Psalm 23:1-3).

4. Some Forms Of Light Activate Creativity

It has been found that some forms of light activate the imagination within certain people. Shining metals and the beaming prisms of crystal, along with the rich texture of other reflective materials, create a sense of enlightenment in an atmosphere. One of the most astonishing things to behold is the sunlight reflected upon the crystal waters of a lake, or the sparkling, white glistening of fresh snow. Let there be light! *"...the sun of righteousness will rise with healing in its wings. And you will go out and leap like calves released from the stall"* (Malachi 4:2).

5. The Sound Of Your Words Creates Realities

Speak to your atmosphere! Speak words of life. Speak words of healing. Speak words filled with encouragement and expectancy. There are warnings all throughout the Scriptures to guard your mouth and be very careful with the words that you speak, because they are powerful in shaping your realities. (See Psalm 141:3, Proverbs 12:13 and Proverbs 13:3.)

Jesus Christ said that his words were *"spirit and life"* (John 6:63). There is a creative life-force behind every word that you speak. Choose your words carefully because they are seeds that will grow a harvest. Do not be surprised by the results they provide. You will reap your harvest according to whatever seeds you have sown. *"But I tell you that men will have to give account on the day of judgment for every careless word they have spoken. For by your words you will be acquitted, and by your words you will be condemned"* (Matthew 12:36-37).

6. Every Color In The Rainbow Is Found Within Light

According to scientific studies, white light is the effect of combining the visible colors of light in equal proportions. God's brilliance is the purest form of light and contains every color of the glory realm. This includes colors that we're familiar with, as well as colors that we've never seen before. We shouldn't be surprised to discover that colors have an impact on our emotional and physical well-being. *"Jesus spoke again to the people, he said, 'I am the light of the world. Whoever follows me will never walk in darkness, but will have the light of life'"* (John 8:12).

7. The Sound Of Music Can Create A Prophetic Atmosphere

Within the Scriptures we can see that the sound of the harpist's music established an excellent setting for Elisha to see into the supernatural realm and he began to prophesy. Oftentimes, anointed worship will produce a clarity in the atmosphere to see and declare the divine purposes of God. The key is having ears to hear the sound of heaven and the skillful ability to play it. *"While the harpist was playing, the hand of the Lord came upon Elisha"* (2 Kings 3:15).

8. The Sound Of Glory Produces Miraculous Change

When the storm raged on the sea, Jesus stood up and fearlessly declared *"peace be still"* (Mark 4:39). When the Centurion's paralyzed servant needed healing, Jesus spoke the Word and it was done (Matthew 8:8-9,13). He even boldly commanded, *"Lazarus, come forth,"* and the dead body raised up with resurrection power (John 11:43-44)! Every sound filled with the glory of God will cause miraculous changes to transpire. *"Jesus replied, "I tell you the truth, if you have faith and do not doubt, not only can you do what was done to the fig tree, but also you can say to this mountain, 'Go, throw yourself into the sea,' and it will be done. If you believe, you will receive whatever you ask for in prayer"* (Matthew 21:21-22).

"Arise, shine, for your light has come, and the glory of the Lord rises upon you" (Isaiah 60:1).

Learning More

Spiritually speaking, we always travel at the speed of light. Your acceleration is determined by your illumination. I have written about the spiritual aspects of God's light and the way it correlates to our atmosphere in *The School Of Miracles, Vol. 1*. If you are interested in learning more about this and furthering your understanding of the miracle realm, I would highly recommend that you get a copy of that school.

Recommended Resources:

- *SpiritSpa Instrumental Piano,* Music CD (Item #CD-11)
- *SpiritSpa 2,* Music CD (Item #CD-21)
- *The School Of Miracles – Vol. 1,* Book (Item #BK-14)

Chapter 5

Colors

*"When Jesus spoke again to the people, he said,
"I am the light of the world. Whoever follows me
will never walk in darkness, but will have
the light of life."*

John 8:12

IN THE BEGINNING WHEN GOD SPOKE, "Let there be light," He spoke into existence every single color in the color spectrum. This includes colors that we can see and even colors that we have yet to discover.

Warm colors (including red, orange and yellow) evoke emotions ranging from feelings of warmth and comfort, to feelings of anger and hostility. Cool colors (including blue, purple and green) are often described as calm, but can also call to mind feelings of sadness or indifference.

In the Old Testament, the significant color of the stones on the priest's breast piece were symbolic of the colors around God's heavenly throne and also represented the colors of the twelve tribes of Israel (Exodus 28:17-21). We can see beautiful colors displayed once again through the jewels in the foundation walls of the New Jerusalem (Revelation 21:18-20). Colors are important to God and display characteristics of His beauty.

Colors are important to God and display characteristics of His beauty.

As you will see below, the colors in your atmosphere will magnify your emotional strengths or weaknesses. By using the proper colors in your environment, you can build a physical atmosphere that will motivate you and allow your inner spirit to be at rest in the presence of the Lord.

Red

Red is the color to which we pay the most attention. It is one of the most demanding colors that commands attention and encourages you towards bold action. This is why it is often used as a stoplight, a stop sign, and for signaling danger. It is the warmest and most energetic color in the spectrum. This is why it is not a good suggestion for bedrooms, hospitals, psychiatric wards, or prisons, because it is too active.

The color red can affect you physically by stimulating the body and mind, increasing your enthusiasm, respiration, heartbeat, circulation and pulse rate. It has also been discovered that people placed in a red room will have an increase of blood pressure and possibly feelings of anger and aggression. *The color red can affect your emotional attitude by providing a sense of protection from fears and anxiety, and it can also influence the stability of your physical health.*

Orange

Orange is a vibrant, flamboyant and warm color that contains luminous qualities. Often recognized for attention-getting purposes, it is usually used on caution signs and in construction zones for safety gear.

Orange is a very active color that stimulates activity and studies show it increases appetites. This is why it is the wrong color for a bedroom, classroom or church sanctuary, but it is a great color for a kitchen, hallway, dining room or living room. The color orange also encourages socialization and conversation. *The color orange can affect your emotional attitude, conversation and appetite.*

Yellow

Yellow is the happiest color in the spectrum, creating a sense of joy, cheerfulness and optimism. The right shade will lift our spirits and self-esteem, although it is also possible for other shades of yellow to create feelings of frustration and anger. Oddly enough, people are more likely to lose their tempers in yellow rooms and babies tend to cry more in yellow rooms.

Studies have shown that the color yellow is a good choice for activating memory, stimulating the imagination, the nervous system and exciting mental processes. It is also a good color for increasing the body's metabolism! *The color yellow can affect your emotional attitude, imagination and physical body.*

Green

Green is a cool color that contains soothing and calming qualities that helps aid in the healing process.

This is why it is often worn in operating rooms by surgeons and is sometimes the color of choice on hospital walls. It has been reported that people that work in a green environment experience fewer stomach aches.

The color green offers a sense of renewal, harmony and self-control as it is the symbol of nature (trees, plants, grass, etc.) and can be used for mental and physical relaxation. Located in the center of the color spectrum, it is the color of balance. The color green helps alleviate depression, nervousness and anxiety. Certain shades are a good choice for living rooms, bedrooms and areas of rest.

Researchers have also discovered that the color green can improve reading ability. According to some studies, students may find that laying a transparent sheet of green paper over reading material increases reading speed and comprehension. *The color green can affect your emotional attitude, health and your quality of relaxation.*

Blue

Blue is a soothing and intelligent color. It is considered to be a business color because it reflects reliability and trust. The strong end of this color spectrum is very uplifting and stimulates clear thought, while the lighter end could possibly calm the mind and aid concentration. Studies also show that people are often more productive while working in offices painted blue.

When using this color you must be careful to avoid any shades which may be too sedating, causing people to feel sad, depressed or dreary. Some studies have found that the color blue can lower the pulse rate and body temperature. Blue is also one of the least appetizing colors, and for this reason some weight-loss plans even recommend eating food off of a blue plate. *The color blue can affect your emotional attitude, health and overall well-being.*

Pink

Pink is a happy, lively and joyful color that encourages friendliness and discourages aggression. This is why some sports teams choose to use pink to color the locker rooms used by the opposing teams, as it has a tranquilizing effect. It is also sometimes used in prison cells to calm inmates.

Some studies suggest that male weight lifters lose up to one third of their strength while exercising in a pink room, while the performance of female weight lifters improves. Scientific studies have also shown that the color pink makes people crave sugar. This is why many donuts and pastries are often packaged in pink boxes. *The color pink can affect your emotional attitude, strength and appetite.*

Purple

Purple is a contemplative color that reflects on spiritual values and encourages deep meditation. It has the ability to calm the mind and nerves while supporting creativity.

In the past, this color has been associated with royalty, wealth and riches as the ancient dyes were much more difficult to attain for use in fashions and makeup. *The color purple can affect your emotional attitude, your sense of value and calmness.*

Colors Affect Our Atmosphere

All of the information about colors that has been compiled within these pages is only touching the tip of the iceberg in comparison with the revelation that God is unfolding. I have done extensive research and study in this area, even exploring the prophetic meaning of colors, and the relationship between colors, sound and healing. I have written several full-color ministry cards that explore these revelations even further, and I would encourage you to obtain them if you are interested in learning more about this.

It's amazing how much colors affect our atmosphere and impact so many different aspects of our lives.

"And it shall come to pass, when I bring a cloud over the earth, that the bow shall be seen in the cloud: And I will remember my covenant, which is between me and you and every living creature of all flesh; and the waters shall no more become a flood to destroy all flesh. And the bow shall be in the cloud; and I will look upon it, that I may remember the everlasting covenant between God and every living creature of all flesh that is upon the earth" (Genesis 9:14-16).

When the Lord created the colors of the rainbow and placed them in the sky as a sign for Noah and his family to see, the message to all of humanity was the goodness of God's promises and His covenant of life. God wants to touch every part of who we are – spirit, soul and body. His colors remind us of this promise.

Recommended Resources:

- *Colors, Sound & Healing,* Ministry Card (Item #MC-03)
- *Prophetic Understanding Of Colors & Numbers,* Ministry Card (Item #MC-04)

Chapter 6

Organization

"Jesus entered the temple area and drove out all who were buying and selling there. He overturned the tables of the money changers and the benches of those selling doves. 'It is written,' he said to them, 'My house will be called a house of prayer,' but you are making it a 'den of robbers.'"

Matthew 21:12-13

WHEN CONSIDERING YOUR ATMO-
SPHERE, organization plays a very important role. If you are disorganized it
will hinder your productivity, your creativity and ultimately your success. Disorganization can also affect the
ability for somebody to receive from the Lord.

The passage of Scripture in Matthew 22 says that
Jesus Christ drove out the money changers and the
people that were creating a disorganized and chaotic
atmosphere at the temple. This atmosphere hindered
people from recognizing that God's house was a place
for prayer and healing.

There have been times when I have ministered in
churches that were completely disorganized. The platform was covered with microphone wires and electrical
cables, and used tissues and tissue boxes were scattered
all across the room. Empty water bottles and miscellaneous papers lay disheveled across a pulpit marked with
greasy handprints.

Now, these things may seem very miniscule to you
in comparison to the greatness of the power of God –
and you're right, they are. But, I have found through my
years of ministry that it's the littlest things that make
the biggest impact.

When I am in a church service and I see these things, it distracts me from the focus of praising the Lord and makes me want to go and clean it up myself. I almost feel embarrassed for the pastors and leaders that would represent their church to other people in this disorderly way.

When you understand that we are created spirit, soul and body, you will begin to recognize the importance of creating an atmosphere that calms the mind and settles the spirit. (I have a detailed teaching on this topic in my lesson "Building The Realm Of Glory" in my *School of Signs & Wonders, Course II*).

Something simple like cleaning the pulpit and picking up all the trash on the platform will reflect well on the ministry. When the stage appears to be organized, it will allow those entering into the room to feel at peace and ready to receive whatever the Lord has for them.

The Lord entrusts us with His work, and expects that we will be diligent in pursuing His presence in everything that we do.

If there is an atmosphere of agitation created through laziness and lack of excellence, it cannot be blamed on the Spirit of God. The Lord entrusts us with His work, and expects that we will be diligent in pursuing His presence in everything that we do.

During those situations where I have encountered cluttered and disorganized atmospheres, I have always felt as though the effectiveness of my ministry was hindered. Unfortunately, the people that came to receive from the Lord were only able to receive in a limited measure because of the natural limitations that had been created through disorganization.

You may think that I'm making a big deal about nothing, but haven't you noticed these same things in your home? When your home is organized you are able to work more efficiently, become more productive, and your days are filled with the blessings of accomplishment.

I've noticed that if my office is filled with papers, unfiled invoices and documents, piles of boxes and random items, it becomes much more difficult to stay focused on the task at hand. It's important for me to organize my priorities, organize my files, organize my relationships and organize my home in order for me to create an atmosphere for success.

Here are four tips for creating an organized atmosphere that will allow you to succeed in developing and maintaining a realm of glory.

1. Organize Your Priorities

I've found that my greatest days of accomplishment are always attained whenever I organize my priorities by creating a daily "To-Do List." I list in order the goals I desire to achieve, even if it won't realistically be possible for me to meet all my goals in one day. Many times I've become pleasantly surprised by how much I accomplished because I gave myself a vision for it.

The famous artist, Michelangelo, once said, "The greater danger is not that your hopes are too high and you fail to reach them; it's that they're too low and you do." Organize your priorities by writing down your work, goals, chores, dreams and assignments that need to be accomplished.

2. Organize Your Relationships

I have found that it's important for me to intentionally organize and prioritize my relationships. I must make a schedule for phone calls, emails and other reminders that allow me to stay connected with those I love and cherish. If I leave my relationships unattended to, oftentimes people will begin to think that I am ignoring them or no longer want to be associated with them. While in reality, my life often becomes so busy that I just simply become too overwhelmed with daily work and administration details, and it becomes easy to forget about friendships.

Relationships are a key for success. They are able to open up new doors of opportunity and create the right atmosphere for you to flourish.

I am still learning how to manage this area better. Relationships are important. Relationships are a key for success. Relationships are able to open up new doors of opportunity and create the right atmosphere for you to flourish.

Organize your relationships by priority. My relationship with God is paramount (Matthew 6:6). Everything in my life flows from a devoted relationship to Him. After that, my family always comes first. I am never too busy to attend to a family need or concern. My closest friends come next and then my business and ministry associations follow.

3. Organize Your Home

An organized home is a happy home. This is your place of refuge and rest. If your home is cluttered and filled with distractions, it will be harder for you to be at rest anywhere else that you go. Organize your kitchen, your living room, your bedroom and your bathroom. You may need to set a few days aside in your schedule to do this. I have found that I am more motivated and encouraged to organize when I'm listening to vibrant praise music. Find out what motivates you to be organized.

You need to create a healthy environment for growing into your fullest potential. Give away all your unused clothing, toys, furniture, books, etc., to your local church or a Christian charity. There are many people that would love to receive them – and they have much more room for them than you do! I have learned to do this at least four times a year. It's amazing how many things you can accumulate over the course of a few short months.

Sort your pictures, miscellaneous items, stored clothing and household supplies into containers that are clearly labeled, and are able to be stored properly in closets and cupboards. If your home is organized, you will begin to feel much better about yourself. As the popular saying goes, "Everything begins at home."

4. Organize Your Computer And Files

Having an organized filing cabinet and an organized computer will save you so much wasted time and effort. Whenever somebody asks you for an important document from the past it will only be a few clicks away or one open drawer from being found.

In our ministry office we have used a simple "F.R.A.T." system for dealing with all incoming emails. We use one of these four options whenever receiving correspondence: File It, Reply To It, Assign It, or Trash It. Organizing your computer and files will help you in creating an atmosphere for success.

Recommended Resources:

- *Let's Get High*, Music CD (Item #CD-08)
- *Time & Eternity*, Book (Item #BK-16)

Chapter 7

Generosity

"A generous man will prosper; he who refreshes others will himself be refreshed."

Proverbs 11:25

D ID YOU KNOW THAT THE WORDS *give*, *giving* and *gave* are mentioned over thirteen hundred times in the King James Version of the Holy Bible? I believe that God has a lot to say to us through His Word in regards to financial matters. The Spirit of Glory is the Spirit of Generosity!

I have discovered that one of the greatest ways to break through an atmosphere of poverty, oppression and lack is by releasing generosity into the middle of it. A few years ago as I was ministering in Riga, Latvia, I began preaching God's truth about prosperity and victory in the area of finances. In my spirit I could sense that there had been an oppressive spirit that had attempted to keep the beautiful Latvian people bound from this revelation. Night after night as the miracles were flowing and God was displaying marvelous signs and wonders in our midst, I continued to preach about supernatural provision and the importance of "sowing into the glory realm."

What an amazing time we had! As the people received the revelation, they began to respond by bringing their offerings and gifts as a generous sacrifice to the work of the Lord. This kind of sacrificial giving triggered something in the Spirit and people began experiencing financial miracles!

In the midst of this generosity there were, of course, a few people who got upset that we were preaching this message of freedom, because a religious spirit will always attempt to keep people bound in chains of lack. But overall, the victories we shared together during that time were just outstanding!

A religious spirit will always try to keep people bound in chains of lack.

Several weeks later Pastor Nikolay sent a wonderful letter to me. In it he said,

> "In our hearts we have vast thankfulness and appreciation for your dedication, fearlessness and courage in serving God. The Glory & Fire Conference in Latvia happened to become a catalyst. We believe that God's Glory and love have been revealed as never before. It was not a regular Christian conference, it was a revolution of faith, revolution of joy and revolution of God's love! There are hundreds of people who were encouraged, set free, healed and anointed by God through your ministry. We are still receiving testimonies about God's glory. The Holy Spirit brought an atmosphere of freedom from human control and religious grief. Now we are tasting

a real spiritual juvenescence in worship and prayers."

The connection between generous giving and the atmosphere of glory is obvious within the Scriptures:

- God's first instruction to Moses for building the tabernacle in the wilderness, was to receive an offering for the Shekinah Glory to reside within that atmosphere (Exodus 25:1-9).

- When David restored the Ark of the Covenant to Jerusalem, God called for generous offerings and extravagant giving (2 Samuel 6:17).

- Great power and grace was released to the early church as they gave generously at the feet of the Apostles (Acts 4:32-35).

Within this book, I have been teaching you the basic concepts of creating an atmosphere in the environment where you live.

Generosity destroys poverty and releases plenty.

You have learned that sound destroys silence and releases creativity, light destroys darkness and releases life, healing destroys sickness and releases wholeness, generosity destroys poverty and releases plenty.

7 Truths About An Atmosphere Of Generosity

1. Generosity Creates An Atmosphere For Multiplication

When the young boy gave his lunch of five loaves and two small fishes into the hands of Jesus, it became the catalyst for multiplication and fed five thousand men (Matthew 14:13-21). When the widow gave her last meal to the Prophet Elijah, it released an abundant supply of food in her home. When you give generously into the glory realm, you create a supernatural atmosphere for multiplication.

Generosity is the motivation for multiplication! *"Elijah said to her, "Don't be afraid. Go home and do as you have said. But first make a small cake of bread for me from what you have and bring it to me, and then make something for yourself and your son. For this is what the Lord, the God of Israel, says: 'The jar of flour will not be used up and the jug of oil will not run dry until the day the Lord gives rain on the land'"* (1 Kings 17:13-14).

> When you give generously into the glory realm, you create a supernatural atmosphere for multiplication.

2. Generosity Releases An Atmosphere Of Love

The proof of love's intensity is its willing generosity. The only way to receive love is by giving it away. Whenever love is present, success is always guaranteed because God's love never fails (1 Corinthians 13:8). I have found that my giving is not under compulsion or because of someone else's persuasion, but the more I fall in love with Jesus the more I want to give into the salvation of souls, healing of lives and the ability to reach the world with the good news of the gospel.

When you are truly touched by the glory of God's love, generosity becomes contagious. *"For God so loved the world that he gave his one and only Son, that whoever believes in him shall not perish but have eternal life"* (John 3:16).

3. Generosity Opens Up The Door For Unusual Blessings

Giving is simply faith in action, reaching out to receive the grace that only God provides. Last year as I was ministering in Houston, Texas, a lady in the meeting was believing God for a miracle breakthrough in her finances. That night she sowed a financial seed of $100 into the offering. She wrote back a few days later with a testimony that her $14,000 hospital bill had been completely forgiven! She received a miracle breakthrough of supernatural debt cancellation.

In our ministry we have had a special anointing for these kinds of money miracles with thousands of testimonies from people who have received unusual blessings from God. One lady in Tampa, Florida, sowed seed into the glory and almost immediately her husband received an unexpected bonus of $2,000 in his job! Generosity opens up the gate for unlimited favor to flow into your life. I like to declare that "my generosity creates an atmosphere for possibility." *Do not be deceived: God cannot be mocked. A man reaps what he sows"* (Galatians 6:7).

4. Generosity Opens Up The Door For Unusual Encounters

In Acts 10, the Bible tells us about a generous man named Cornelius who was part of the Italian army. He gave alms to those in need and prayed to God regularly and his whole family was devout and God-fearing. In the Scriptures we read about an amazing encounter where an angel appeared one afternoon because of Cornelius' generosity in giving. The angel said, "Your gifts to the poor have come up as a memorial offering before God."

Not only did Cornelius experience a glorious encounter with an angel because of his generosity, but the Scriptures go on to tell us that Cornelius and his entire household, relatives and close-friends received the baptism in the Holy Spirit (along with the evidence of speaking in tongues) as Peter was sent to them to preach the gospel. And it all began with a generous gift (Acts

10:30-46). *"A gift opens the way for the giver and ushers him into the presence of the great"* (Proverbs 18:16).

5. Generosity Destroys An Atmosphere Of Poverty

A spirit of generosity is always a threat to a withholding spirit of lack. I am never ashamed to receive offerings or talk about financial blessing, because I have found in my own life that the key to living a debt-free life is obtained by becoming a generous giver in my finances. When other ministers are embarrassed to receive an offering, I oftentimes wonder what they are embarrassed about? What are they planning on doing with the money that makes them so distressed?

I am never embarrassed to talk about finances publicly from the pulpit because I see the great need in the nations for financial deliverance. I will always give an opportunity for people to sow into the glory realm, because it's when you enter into that cycle of seedtime and harvest that you begin to partake of an extraordinary miracle.

I have applied this principle in my own life and I purpose to be a generous giver. Janet Angela and I have given away computers, keyboards, vehicles, designer watches and countless finances and we have been given the same in return. The truth is, the more I hold back, the more that is held back from me. The more I give, the more I receive. It is a spiritual principle that will always work.

In our meetings, people have experienced multiplication of money, debt reduction and many other amazing miracles in regards to finances. One lady was preparing to give some money in the offering at a recent meeting, and just like the fishes and loaves, the money multiplied in her hand and suddenly she was holding more! Some people have found that it has multiplied almost instantly in their wallets, purses and even in their bank accounts. (I have shared more detailed testimonies of supernatural financial provision in my book, *Positioned For Prosperity*.) You can never out-give God. He is so extravagant in His giving. *"One man gives freely, yet gains even more; another withholds unduly, but comes to poverty"* (Proverbs 11:24).

> *The truth is, the more I hold back, the more that is held back from me.*

6. Generosity Creates An Atmosphere Of Provision

Many students at our Intensified Glory Institute® have experienced the multiplication of money as twenty-dollar bills have appeared supernaturally. For some, the money appeared in their purses and wallets without natural reason, and for Marylou in Palm Springs, these twenty-dollar bills appeared on the floor after she was obedient to give some money to a fellow student, as she was directed by the Lord. Seeing these miracles happen has been so faith building and encouraging, realizing that God's economic situation doesn't look anything like the natural economy.

Whenever we purpose in our heart to be generous, there is always a new realm of provision on the other side of our gift. One student shared this testimony.

> "Upon the first week after the Intensified Glory Institute, my employer provided the Managers (I included) an unexpected raise of $4,000 more a year! I know after Joshua had decreed blessings to us, for new jobs, promotions, increase, the Lord had it happen at that point of time of declaration. Believe me, I nor did the others expect it, especially after the serious recession we had encountered.... Praise be to God, that not only did we survive the worst time, but business is on the rise and we are hiring again."

"Now he who supplies seed to the sower and bread for food will also supply and increase your store of seed and will enlarge the harvest of your righteousness" (2 Corinthians 9:10).

7. Extravagant Generosity Builds An Atmosphere Filled With Extravagant Outpouring

At the dedication of Solomon's Temple, great sacrifice was given through generous gifts, musical expression, and voices lifted in praise. Following the extravagant giving came a tremendous outpouring of God's manifest glory, as the visible cloud of His presence filled the temple to such a degree that the ministers became transfixed by the awe of His splendor!

We have witnessed some of the greatest miracles in our own lives following times of great sacrifice and extravagant giving. *"King Solomon and the entire assembly of Israel that had gathered about him were before the ark, sacrificing so many sheep and cattle that they could not be recorded or counted... Then the temple of the Lord was filled with a cloud, and the priests could not perform their service because of the cloud, for the glory of the Lord filled the temple of God"* (2 Chronicles 5:6,13-14).

Recommended Resources:

- *Positioned For Prosperity,* Book (Item #BK-15)
- *Kingdom Economics In The Glory Realm,* Ministry Card (Item #MC-13)
- *Proverbs Of Prosperity,* Ministry Card (Item #MC-14)

- *7 Keys For Living In Abundance,* Ministry Card (Item #MC-15)
- *Miracle Money,* Teaching CD (Item #CD-14)

Chapter 8

Influencing Your Environment

"Therefore everyone who hears these words of mine and puts them into practice is like a wise man who built his house on the rock."

Matthew 7:24

I T'S TIME TO PUT THESE TRUTHS INTO AC-
TION! Throughout this book I have been sharing
personal revelations with you that I have learned
about creating a realm for miracles and success in my
own life. As I have set these truths into motion, I have
found a greater fruitfulness flowing in my life and ministry with an increased sensitivity to the manifest presence of the Lord.

God has called you for a life of miracles and success
too!

As you become aware of how your spirit, soul and
body are moved by spiritual, emotional and physical
things – you can determine to create an environment
that will cause you to flourish in the things of God and
cause you to pursue His tangible presence.

God wants you to influence your environment. You
can become a catalyst for the glory of God everywhere
you go! You see, light is stronger than darkness. Life is
more forceful than death. Peace is more powerful than
war, and love is more tenacious than hate. In the Spirit
you have been given everything you will ever need to
shift the atmosphere around you. Just as Jesus Christ
prayed in Matthew 6:10, I believe that God wants to use
you to bring the atmosphere of heaven to earth!

*"I have given them your word and the world
has hated them, for they are not of the world*

any more than I am of the world. My prayer is not that you take them out of the world but that you protect them from the evil one. They are not of the world, even as I am not of it. Sanctify them by the truth; your word is truth. As you sent me into the world, I have sent them into the world." (John 17:14-18)

The Scriptures tell us that we can be in this world, but that we don't necessarily need to be a part of its ways. You have the marvelous ability to influence your environment with the ways of heaven. You can participate with a greater flow. You can partake of a miracle realm that is not restricted to the laws of the natural. You can live in a dimension of success that is unparalleled to anything you have ever known before.

Your atmosphere is important to God. You were created in an atmosphere of glory and God has always intended for you to live and walk in that dimension of supernatural life! I encourage you to walk in these truths and allow them to flow out of you with hope, healing and divine success!

It All Begins With Jesus Christ

In order to influence your atmosphere with life-changing power, you must have a personal relationship with Jesus Christ. Do you know Him? The Bible says:

> *That if you confess with your mouth, "Jesus is Lord," and believe in your heart that God raised him from the dead, you will be saved. For it is with your heart that you believe and are justified, and it is with your mouth that you confess and are saved.* (Romans 10:9-10)

If you want to give your life to Christ, pray this with me right now:

> *Father, thank you for forgiving my sins. Jesus, come into my heart. Make me the kind of person You want me to be. Thank you for saving me. Amen.*

The Bible is very clear that *"everyone who calls on the name of the Lord will be saved"* (Romans 10:13). Welcome to the family of God! Please use the contact information on the Resources page to let us know that you have chosen to follow Christ, and we will send you a free gift called "Starting Your New Life" (Item #IT-01) to help you grow strong in your new relationship with Christ.

Now go influence your environment and become a catalyst for the glory of God everywhere you go!

More Resources
from Joshua & Janet Angela Mills

For additional copies of this book, more information about live spiritual training seminars, The Intensified Glory Institute®, and other glory resources, please contact the ministry of Joshua & Janet Angela Mills.

NEW WINE INTERNATIONAL

In USA: PO Box 4037, Palm Springs, CA 92263

Toll-free 1-866-60-NEW-WINE

Online 24/7 www.NewWineInternational.org

Bulk Order Discounts for Ministries, Churches & Christian Retailers:

Discounts are available to all churches, ministries and bookstores that desire to place large quantity orders. For more information please email: product@newwineinternational.org

Books by Joshua Mills

31 Days Of Health, Wealth & Happiness

31 Days To A Breakthrough Prayer Life

31 Days To A Miracle Mindset

Advanced School Of Miracles

Atmosphere

Into His Presence – Praise & Worship Manual

Ministry Resources 101

Personal Ministry Prayer Manual

Positioned For Prosperity

School Of Miracles, Volume I

School Of Miracles, Volume II

School Of Signs & Wonders, Course I

School Of Signs & Wonders, Course II

Simple Supernatural

Simple Supernatural Study Guide

Third Day Prayers

Time & Eternity

Available online 24/7 at:

www.NewWineInternational.org

Dear Friend,

I believe that you are a kingdom connection! God wants to use you to make a difference in the lives of thousands around the world. Do you believe that?

I would like to invite you to become a *Miracle Worker* with me, and help me take this supernatural message of Jesus Christ and His glory to the far corners of the earth.

Partnership is not simply giving of your finances; it is more. When you become a *Miracle Worker* with this ministry, you will become an integral member of the New Wine International outreach ministry team with special opportunities and privileges that will position you to have global impact.

A *"Miracle Worker"* is a person who agrees to:
1. Financially support the ministry of New Wine International (NWI)
2. Pray faithfully for Joshua & Janet Angela Mills and the NWI Ministry Team as they carry the message of Jesus Christ around the world.
3. Pray for those who will receive ministry through NWI ministry events and resources.

Partnership is not only what you can do to help me, but also what I can do to help you. Becoming a *Miracle Worker* with NWI provides a covenant agreement between you and me. By being a *Miracle Worker,* you will connect with the anointing and glory on this ministry as I send you monthly updates and revelatory teachings on the glory realm. You will receive my continued prayer for you and your family and you will be linked with the unique anointing that is on this ministry for unusual signs and wonders.

There are currently several ways to partner with NWI. I want you to decide the partnership level according to what the Lord has placed in your heart to do.

In His Great Love,

Joshua Mills

P.S. *Call my office today to become a partner or register online so that I can send you a special **Miracle Worker** Welcome Package filled with special benefits and information.*

Toll-Free: **1-866-60-NEW-WINE**
Online 24/7:
www.NewWineInternational.org
www.PartnersInPraise.com

Praise for these Best-selling Books...

"Joshua has identified simple, yet profound keys found in the Word of God that will help the reader receive an impartation to unlock the realms of success and happiness..."

- Drs. Christian & Robin Harfouche (Senior Pastors, Miracle Faith Center, Pensacola, FL)

"...31 Days Of Health, Wealth and Happiness is a helpful resource to assist you in your daily walk of faith... we recommend this book to you!"

- Dr. Stephen & Kellie Swisher (Senior Executives, Kenneth Copeland Ministries)

"...Joshua Mills brings a faith building truth, a scriptural basis for that truth, a great quote for the day and a reminder of Biblical accounts of the miraculous. Each page will move you toward a miracle mindset that will, in turn, catapult you into the glory realm of God...where nothing is impossible. This book is a must read for anyone who wants to live in a greater dimension of the supernatural."

- Dr. Jeff Walker, D. Min., Psy. D., Licensed Clinical Psychologist

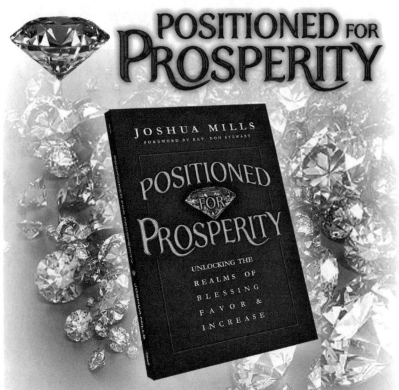

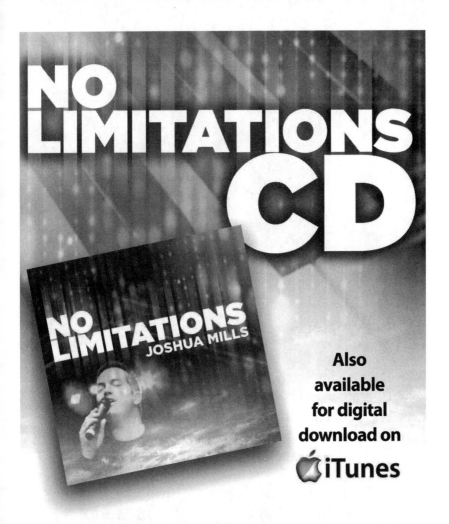

there is no spa like a...

SpiritSpa

rest | ease | rejuvenation

SpiritSpa ▶   ◀ SpiritSpa II

"...times of refreshing shall come from the presence of the Lord."
– Acts 3:19

"...I fully recommend SpiritSpa for every massage therapist as well as anyone else who is looking for music to aid in relaxation."
Melody Barker, NCTM, LMT TX, LMT TN
Nationally Certified Massage Therapist,
Nashville, Tennessee

"...this music does in fact belong in every spa across the country."
Shaun H.,
Radio Indy Music Review,
Encinitas, California

These CDs gently envelop and embrace you in a blanket of restful peace. Linger in heavenly realms and indulge your spirit with these soothing instrumental piano melodies. This beautiful music by Joshua Mills is sure to calm the spirit, soul and body with God's supernatural rest, ease and rejuvenation.

Call Toll-Free To Order Today! 1-866-60-NEW-WINE
www.NewWineInternational.org